Portfoolio 19

THE YEAR'S BEST CANADIAN EDITORIAL CARTOONS

EDITED WITH TEXT BY **GUY BADEAUX**

McArthur & Company

Canadian Cataloguing in Publication Data
Portfoolio: the year in Canadian caricature

Annual.
Subtitle varies.
Imprint varies.
Includes some text in French.
ISSN 0839-6485
ISBN 1-55278-404-5 (volume 19)

1. Canada - Politics and government - 1984-   - Caricatures and cartoons.
2. World politics - Caricatures and cartoons.   3. Canadian wit and humor, Pictorial.   I. Title: Portfolio.

NC1300.P67   971.064'7'0267   C89-030416-5 rev

The publisher would like to acknowledge the financial support of the Government of Canada
through the Book Publishing Industry Development Program, the Canada Council, and the
Ontario Arts Council for our publishing activities. We also acknowledge the Government of
Ontario through the Ontario Media Development Corporation Ontario Book Initiative.

Edited by: **Guy Badeaux**
Text by: **Guy Badeaux**
Guy Badeaux is editorial cartoonist for *Le Droit* in Ottawa.

Design by: **Mathilde Hébert**

Printed and bound in Canada

McArthur & Company
322 King St. West, Suite 402
Toronto, Ontario
M5V 1J2
www.mcarthur-co.com

Art Eggleton gave a $ 36,500. contract to an ex-girlfriend.
– I see nothing wrong with that!

SERGE CHAPLEAU, *La Presse*, Montreal, May 28, 2002

MICHAEL DE ADDER, *The Halifax Daily News*, November 13, 2002

MALCOLM MAYES, *The Edmonton Journal*, September 20, 2002

'THE STATE of THE NATION'..

Oil be back!

Does revenge fuel Dubya or is it just coincidence that he's finishing the war his father started?

Afghanistan had been invaded but the trail to bin Laden was getting frigid. An easier target had to be found in the war on terrorism. Saddam Hussein fitted the bill. He had, or at least was seeking, weapons of mass destruction that could be deployed within 45 minutes and had tried to buy enriched uranium from Niger. Who cared that none of this was true? It had been enough to convince the American public and most of the media that it was the US's duty to topple an evil regime and bring democracy to Iraq.

LIND, Weltschmerz

ZAHARUK

8.

CORRIGAN, *The Toronto Star*

McCLEOD, *The Globe and Mail*

CUMMINGS, *The Winnipeg Free Press*

PERRY

RICE

PERRY

NEASE, *The Oakville Beaver*

MAYES, *The Edmonton Journal*

CLEMENT, *The National Post*

UN inspectors come back empty-handed from Baghdad.

LOTH, *Le Droit*, Ottawa

– Nothing! Proof that it's well hidden!

GARNOTTE, *Le Devoir*, Montreal

JUSQU'OÙ LES INSPECTEURS DE L'ONU FOUILLERONT-ILS?

Just how far will the UN inspectors search?

CHAPLEAU, *La Presse*, Montreal

MAYES, *The Edmonton Journal*

LEFCOURT

PETERSON, *The Vancouver Sun*

PETERSON, *The Vancouver Sun*

TAB , *The Calgary Sun*

The US Congress will replace "French fries" with "freedom fries" in its' cafeterias…

GARNOTTE, *Le Devoir*, Montreal

MURPHY, *The Province*, Vancouver

– Going home?

CÔTÉ, *Le Soleil*, Quebec

LEFCOURT

MOU, *The Toronto Star*

TAB , *The Calgary Sun*

HARROP, *Back Bench*

It's in the bag, dad!

What started out as a high-tech show of force turns into a steady stream of body bags.

If the US had made wild claims before invading Iraq, they would be outdone by the falling regime's PR expert. "What Americans?" he claimed as US tanks could be seen rolling in the background. The fierce resistance that was apprehended did not materialize. At least not before the fall of Baghdad.

Iraqi generals wonder…

– Shouldn't we redecorate?

CÔTÉ, *Le Soleil*, Quebec

BADO, *Le Droit*, Ottawa

MACKINNON, *The Chronicle-Herald*, Halifax

For some reason, our "smart" bombs won't detonate!

GARNOTTE, *Le Devoir*, Montreal

DEA, *La Presse*, Montreal

DEWAR, *Ottawa Sun*

MACKAY, *The Hamilton Spectator*

BADO, *Le Droit*, Ottawa

Americans welcomed with open arms.

BADO, *Le Droit*, Ottawa

with the fall of Baghdad, the looting began in earnest....

SHAHID

ARNOULD, *The Georgia Straight*, Vancouver

MACKAY, *The Hamilton Spectator*

GABLE, *The Globe and Mail*

ROSEN, *Montreal Mirror*

TAB , *The Calgary Sun*

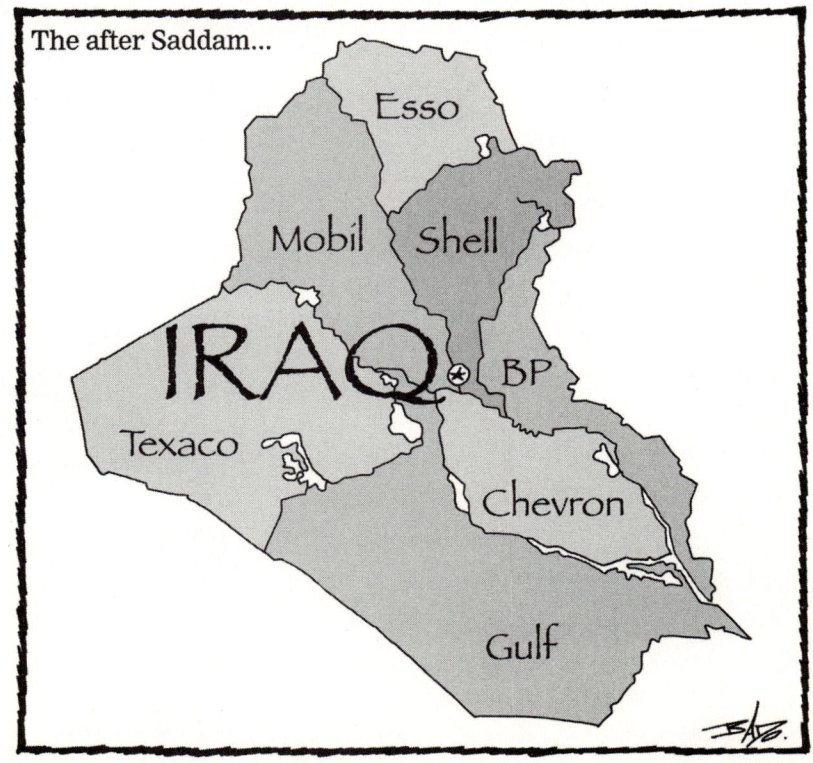

BADO, *Le Droit*, Ottawa

BADO, *Le Droit*, Ottawa

CLEMENT, *The National Post*

PETERSON, *The Vancouver Sun*

CLEMENT, *The National Post*

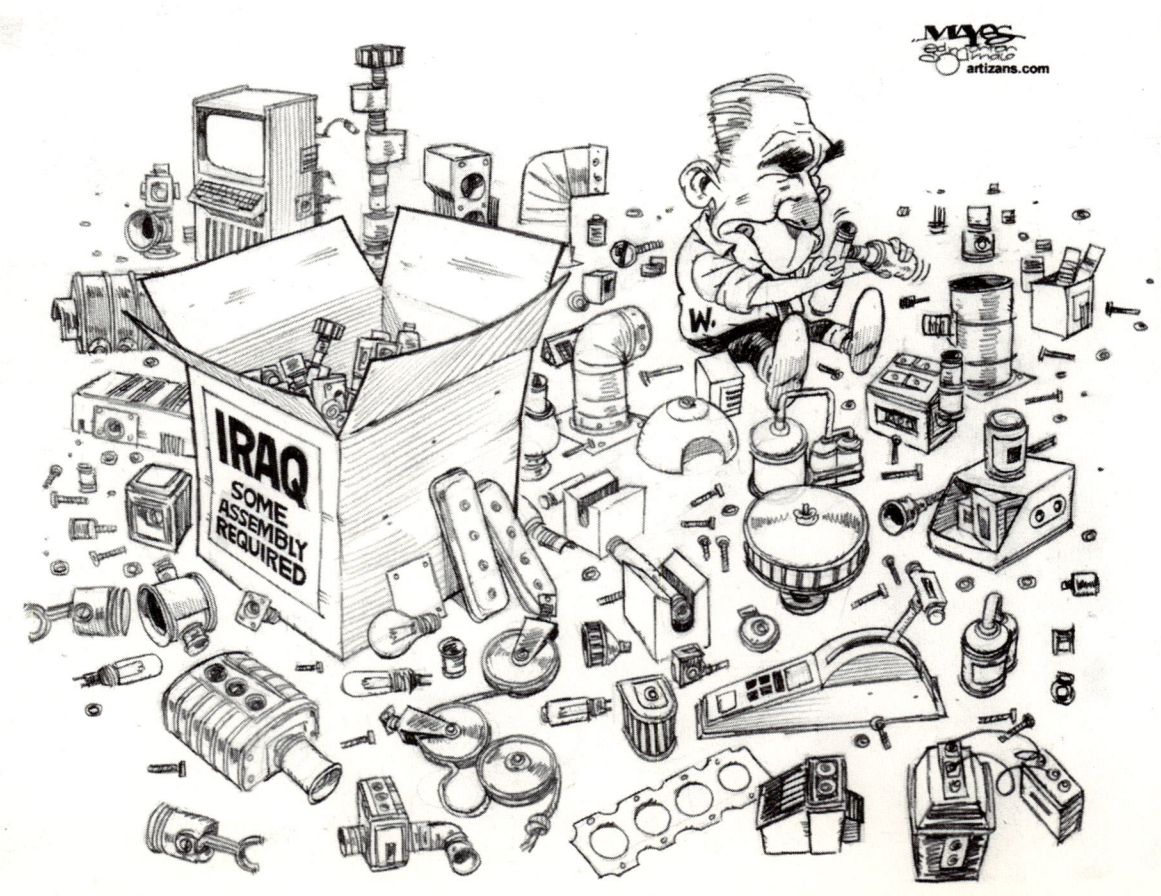

MAYES, *The Edmonton Journal*

Bin there and everywhere

Canada is fingered for lax security despite lending a helping hand.

Osama bin Laden has not been seen on TV for quite a while but audio-tapes keep popping up everywhere. Canada is even mentioned as a potential target. And we thought we were only getting it from the Americans. Four Canadian soldiers were killed by "friendly" fire in Afghanistan and the US pilots responsible for the deed have still not been brought to justice. On the other hand, we should count ourselves lucky that the Sea King helicopter aboard the HMCS Iroquois only fell from a few metres when it crashed after takeoff.

ROSEN, *Montreal Mirror*

PHILLIPS, *The Toronto Sun*

PETERSON, *The Vancouver Sun*

BADO, *Le Droit*, Ottawa

McCLEOD, *The Globe and Mail*

MACKINNON, *The Chronicle-Herald*, Halifax

· CITIZENS ·

CUMMINGS, *The Winnipeg Free Press*

DE ADDER, *Halifax Daily News*

GRASTON, *The Windsor Star*

FRIENDLY FIRE RULING

MAYES, *The Edmonton Journal*

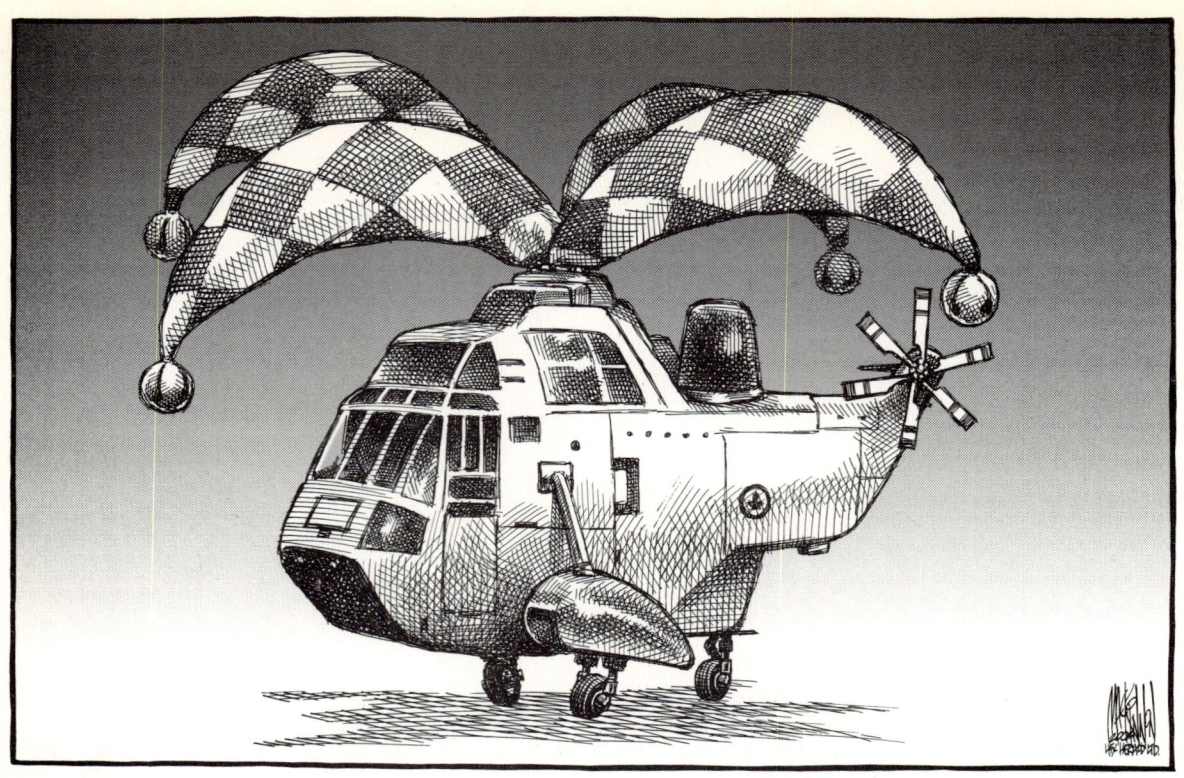

MACKINNON, *The Chronicle-Herald*, Halifax

DE ADDER, *Halifax Daily News*

TAB , *The Calgary Sun*

Libya wil! head the UN's Human Rights Commission.

Missed opportunities

The Miss World contest retreats to friendlier territory and the "roadmap to peace" leads to a dead end.

Yasser Arafat is set aside as the US forces the nomination of a Palestinian prime minister, Mahmoud Abbas, with whom they would rather deal. A cease-fire is brokered only to be broken when suicide bombings lead to targeted assassinations that, in turn, beg for retaliation. It could also be the other way around. Who knows by now?

The Miss World pageant, held in Nigeria because the previous year's winner came from there, is marred by riots provoked, in part, by an article that claimed that the prophet Mohammed would gladly have chosen any of the contestants as his bride. This was seized upon as an excuse for weeklong riots that forced the pageant, as well as the author of the article, to seek refuge in London.

GARNOTTE, *Le Devoir*, Montreal

ON A PEDESTAL

ANDY, *The Globe and Mail*

DEA, *La Presse*, Montreal

.53

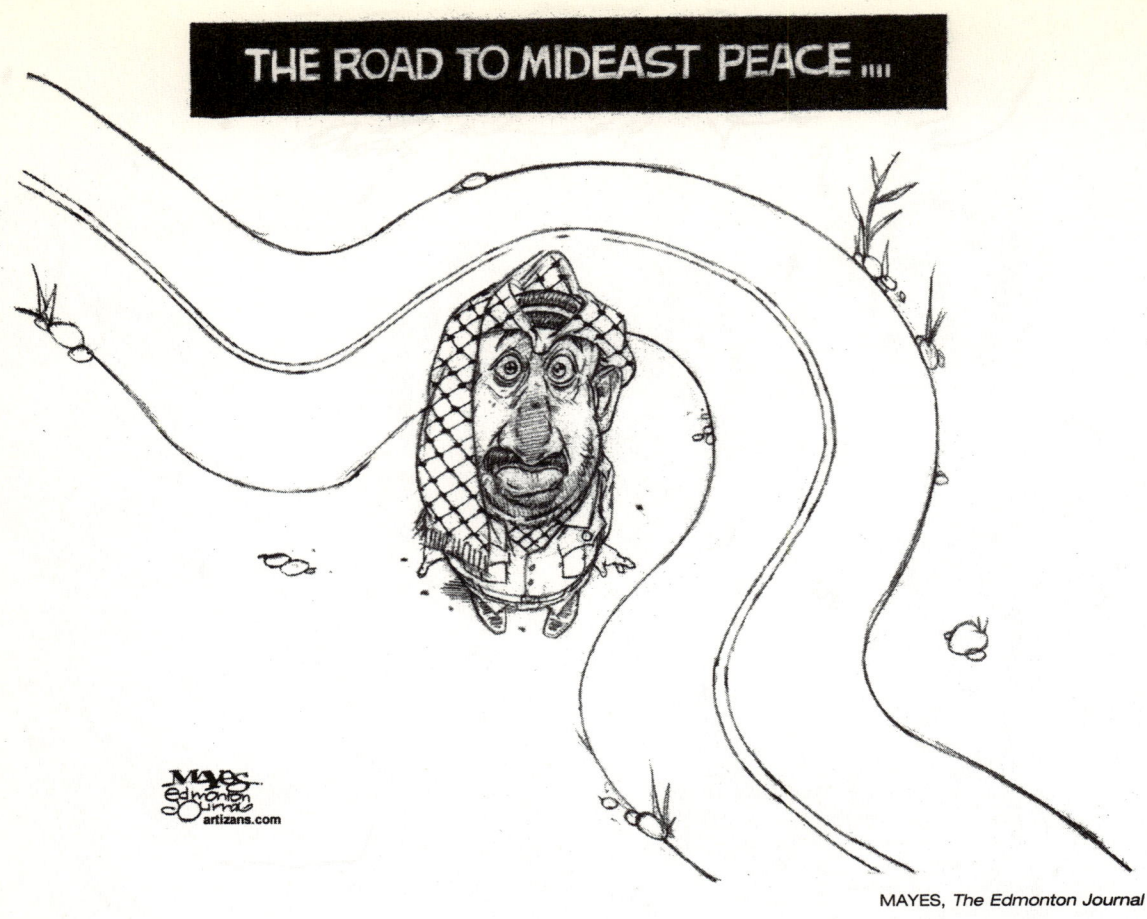

MAYES, *The Edmonton Journal*

RICE

NEASE, *The Oakville Beaver*

PERRY

CLEMENT, *The National Post*

CLEMENT, *The National Post*

PERRY

Then   Now

BADO, *Le Droit*, Ottawa

RICE

DU NIGÉRIA, L'ÉLECTION DE MISS MONDE EST TRANSFÉRÉE À LONDRES

The Miss World pageant is moved from Nigeria to London.

– We must eliminate poverty…

– …Finally live in peace…

– …loving and sharing…

CHAPLEAU, *La Presse*, Montreal

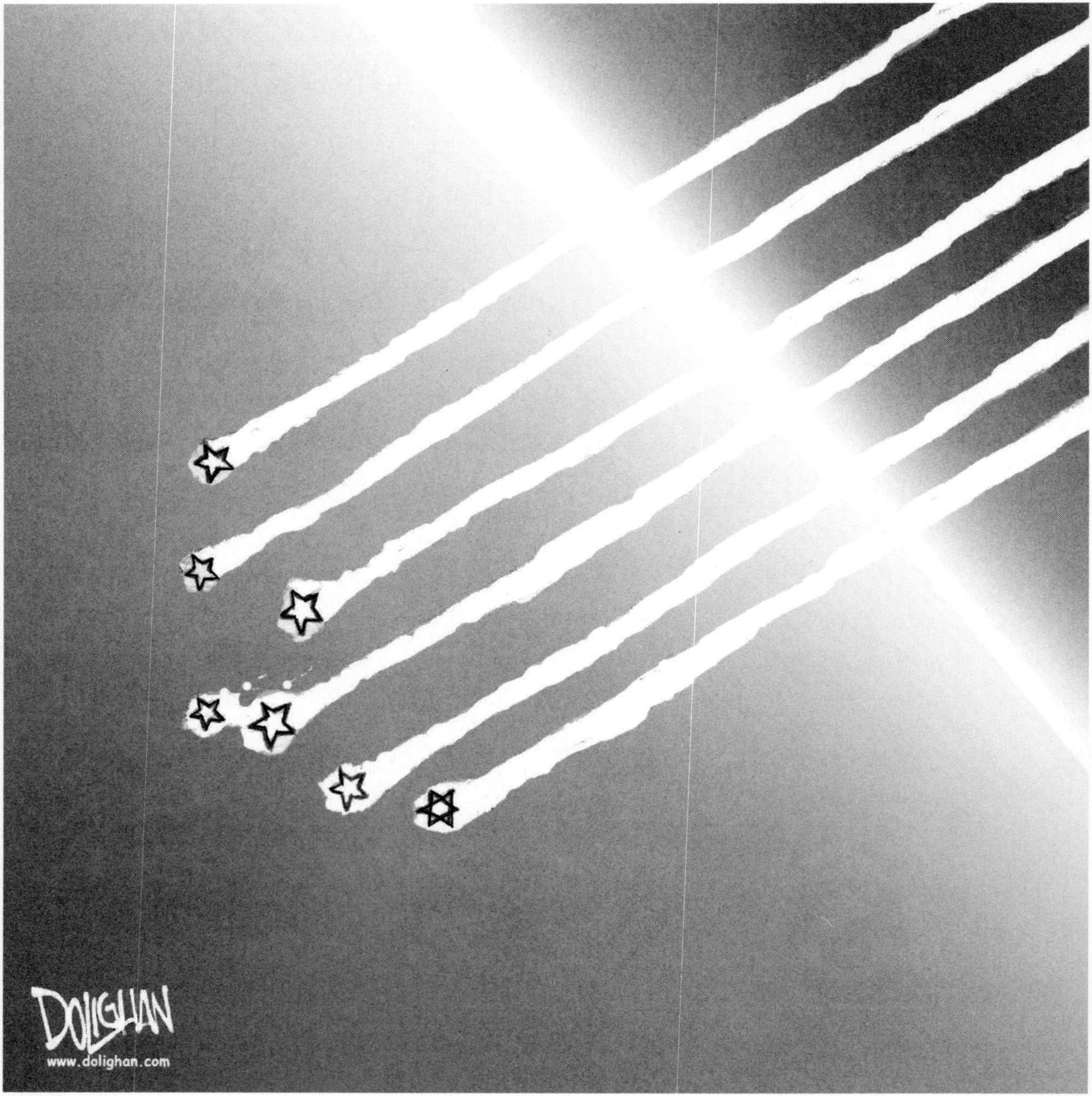

Stars of many stripes

The Columbia space shuttle explodes and fear gripes DC.

A sniper spreads fear in the Washington area and what was first thought to be the act of a terrorist becomes an all-too-common occurrence in the US: a random killing spree. The star of good housekeeping, Martha Stewart, is accused of insider trading. Her good friend Hillary Clinton, another victim of a vast right-wing conspiracy, publishes tell-all memoirs that don't reveal anything new.

Arnold Schwarzenneger announces on the *Tonight Show* that he will be running for governor of California in a recall election likely to displace the Democrat incumbent. Did we mention that Larry Flynt, Gary Coleman and even a porn star are also in the running?

CORRIGAN, *The Toronto Star*

GABLE, *The Globe and Mail*

BORDELEAU, *La Presse*, Montreal

HARROP, *Back Bench*

CORRIGAN, *The Toronto Star*

CUMMINGS, *The Winnipeg Free Press*

WELL IF THIS DOESN'T BOOST THE DOW, NOTHING WILL.

ANDY, *The Globe and Mail*

CELINE DION'S **LAS VEGAS DIARY:**

FEB. 12. I STILL CAN'T BELIEVE HOW MUCH THEY ARE PAYING ME TO DO THIS SHOW! I HAVE ENTRUSTED THE MONEY TO RENÉ ANGÉLIL WHO IS PUTTING IT IN WHAT HE CALLS A 'ROTATING FUND'.

harrop 4-10

$100 MILLION ON BLACK AND THE WHEEL IS SPINNING!

HARROP, *Back Bench*

TAB, *The Calgary Sun*

DE ADDER, *Halifax Daily News*

MAYES, *The Edmonton Journal*

DE ADDER, *Halifax Daily News*

HARROP, *Back Bench*

DEA, *La Presse*, Montreal

HARROP, *Back Bench*

COLE
23·4·3

Now you see them, now you don't

The Pope electrifies a Toronto crowd. Too bad he can't be there all the time.

A sea change occurred in Quebec as the PQ, after three man-dates and as many leaders, loses power to Jean Charest's Liberal party. The city of Vancouver gets the 2010 winter Olympics, dash-ing Toronto's hopes of becoming host to the summer Games in 2012. On August 14th, a major power failure plunges most of east-ern North America into the dark. As this event occurred too late to be included in this book, we'll have cartoons on the subject in *Portfoolio 20.*

BORDELEAU, *La Presse*, Montreal

GRASTON, *The Windsor Star*

CORRIGAN, *The Toronto Star*

THE ROLLING BLACKOUTS

GABLE, *The Globe and Mail*

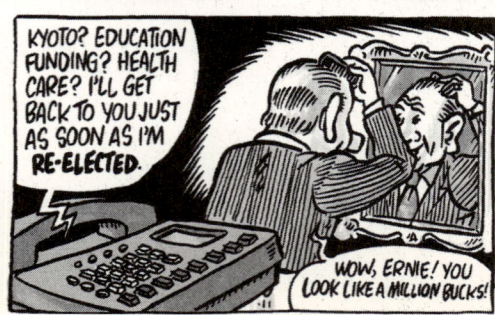

LIND, Weltschmerz

LIFE *After* LIVING OFF THE PUBLIC PURSE...

WHAT'S GOING ON AT TABLE 14?.. THEY'RE TAKING FOREVER TO LEAVE.

OH THAT'S THE CHRIS STOCKWELL-GEORGE RADWANSKI TABLE.... THEY'RE WAITING FOR EACH OTHER TO PICK UP THE CHEQUE.

GRASTON, *The Windsor Star*

HARROP, *Back Bench*

NEASE, *The Oakville Beaver*

Our Possible 2010 Olympics' Demonstration Sports

Downhill Hot-tubbing

The Apres-Ski Pentathlon

The Alpine Cross-Country Recall

murphy * the province

MURPHY, *The Province*, Vancouver

Make that a double!

Clones were sprouting left and right and Gordon Campbell was driving pretty much the same way in Hawaii.

Some strange claims were made last year. A Quebec sect had cloned a girl named Eve born on Christmas Day in an undisclosed location. Or was it three clones? Who's counting? The world would know soon enough. But, since the presumed parents were too shy to identify themselves or the US government was making uncomfortable inquiries, the story quietly died. Either that or the newsrooms came to their senses when the editors returned from holidays.

Another strange claim was that Gordon Campbell had had only one glass of white wine before being arrested for erratic driving during a Hawaiian vacation. But then again, who's counting?

The strangest revelation of all was certainly that Michael Jackson would invite young boys for sleepovers in his mansion and that they would share his bed without their parents being the least bit worried. I guess he told them it was a double bed.

DEWAR, *Ottawa Sun*

HARROP, *The Vancouver Sun*

BORDELEAU, *La Presse*, Montreal

Another good reason to ban...

...human cloning!

BADO, *Le Droit*, Ottawa

← NOT A MORON

AND WHILE WE'RE AT IT

NOT NUTS →

MURPHY, *The Province*, Vancouver

BORDELEAU, *Voir*, Montreal

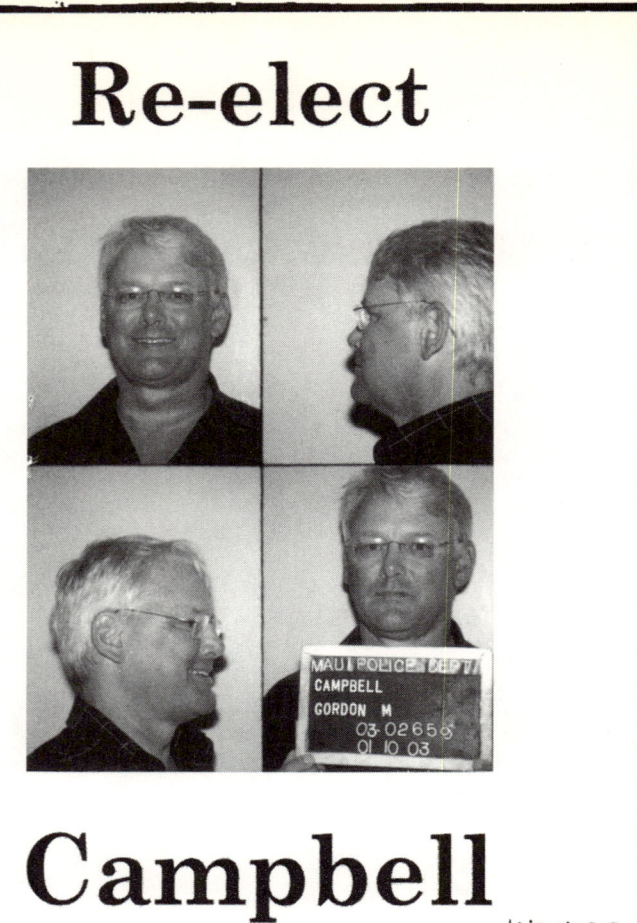

KRIEGER, *The Province*, Vancouver

CORRIGAN, *The Toronto Star*

DEWAR, *The Toronto Sun*

The sky is the limit

We're either talking about George Radwanski's expense account or the gun registry's cost overruns, certainly not the wages paid by Air Canada.

The House of Common's Government Operations and Estimates Committee issues a scorching report declaring non-confidence in the Privacy Commissioner for his lavish expenses and accusing him of deliberately misleading Parliament after it was discovered that he had altered documents with liquid paper.

As for the gun registry, what started out as a 2-million-dollar program has ballooned into something that will cost us close to a billion.

NEASE, *The Oakville Beaver*

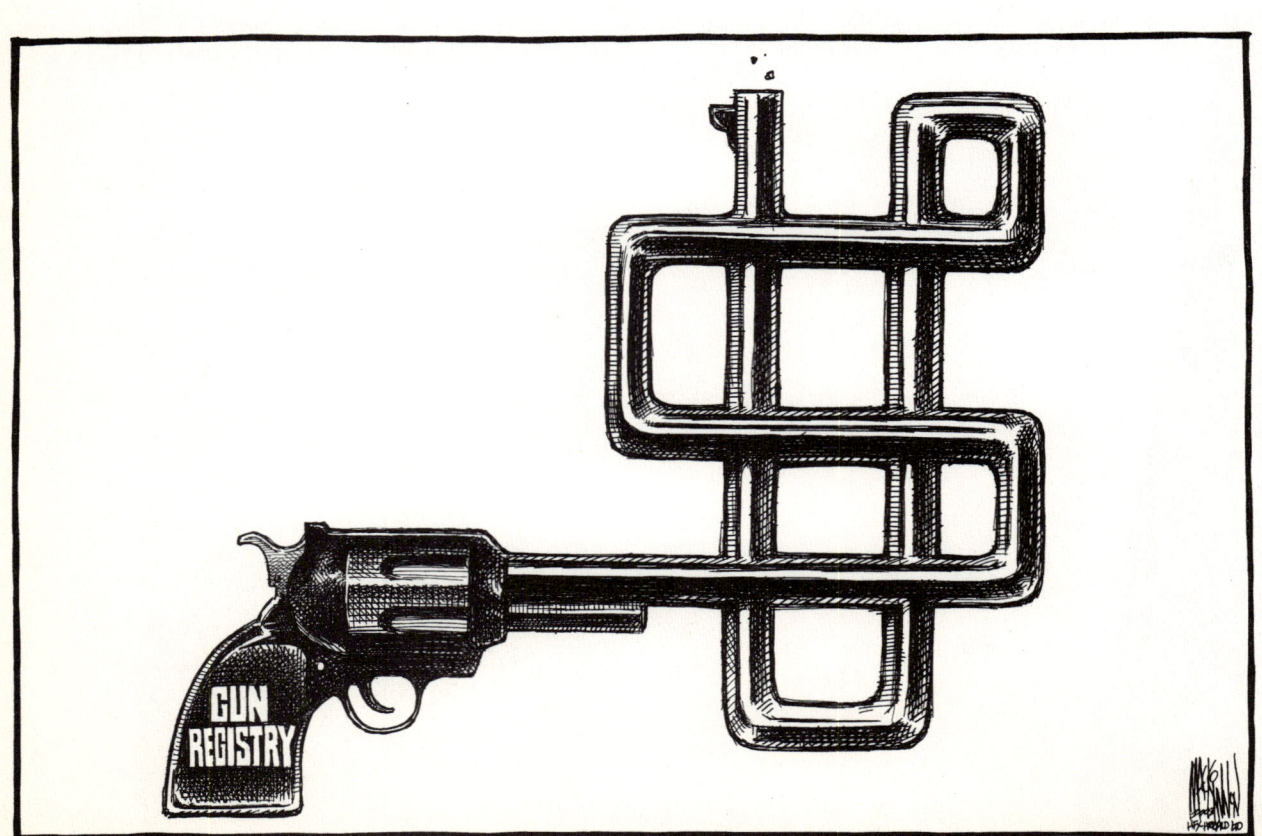

MACKINNON, *The Chronicle-Herald*, Halifax

GABLE, *The Globe and Mail*

TAB , *The Calgary Sun*

THE **Province**

Tooth found in Ethics Watchdog

Doesn't stop at MacAulay Demands resignation of *everyone* in Ottawa

murphy*the province

MURPHY, *The Province*, Vancouver

TAB, *The Calgary Sun*

PASCAL, *Law Times*

CLEMENT, *The National Post*

RADWANSKI ON-A-STICK —

$10,607.8¢

CUMMINGS, *The Winnipeg Free Press*

ADHERING TO THE ANCIENT DICTATES OF BUSHIDO 'CODE OF THE BUREAUCRAT', AN HONOUR-BOUND GEORGE RADWANSKI FALLS ON HIS FORK...

JENKINS, *The Globe and Mail*

GABLE, *The Globe and Mail*

RICE

PETERSON, *The Vancouver Sun*

A Brief History of the Canadian Alliance Party

MURPHY, *The Province*, Vancouver

GABLE, *The Globe and Mail*

ZAHARUK

McCLEOD, *The Globe and Mail*

NEASE, *The Oakville Beaver*

P.C. LEADERSHIP...

Goodbye Joe!

If you think the Progressive Conservative's leadership race was boring, think anew.

Joe Clark was not the only federal party leader who resigned last year. It seems Alexa McDonough also left the scene, leaving Gilles Duceppe of the Bloc Québécois as the longest serving party leader when Jean Chrétien finally departs.

The PC leadership race, much like that of the New Democrats, was a family affair, enlivened only by the fact that one candidate, David Orchard, was running against the North American Free Trade Agreement, Brian Mulroney's proudest legacy.

Did we mention that Jack Layton is now leader of the NDP? So far, he's known for riding a bicycle.

PERRY

KRIEGER, *The Province*, Vancouver

MAYES, *The Edmonton Journal*

OH YOU'RE GOOD, MACKAY. BUT YOU'RE NO JOE CLARK.

MOU, *The Toronto Star*

MACKAY, *The Hamilton Spectator*

AISLIN, *The Gazette*, Montreal

PHILLIPS, *The Toronto Sun*

Emotional Rescue

What started out as a WHO advisory turned into a Rolling Stones concert.

After an outbreak of Severe Acute Respiratory Syndrome hits Toronto, the World Health Organisation issues a travel warning that pretty much cripples the tourism industry.

Since the disease originates in China, Jean Chrétien tries to reassure the public at large by first, eating in a Chinese restaurant and then, holding a cabinet meeting in the city. The clear message being sent out was somewhat blurred when they then called out for pizza.

Meanwhile in most Canadian dailies, the same suggestion was made to their editorial cartoonists: why don't you draw the CN Tower with a surgical mask?

You've been warned.

FEWINGS, *The Peterborough Examiner*

CLEMENT, *The National Post*

WHO issues a travel alert for Toronto…
– Sorry, Jean, I must cancel my visit to Canada…
–…you know how much I respect international organizations!

GARNOTTE, *Le Devoir*, Montreal

MOU, *The Toronto Star*

GRASTON, *The Windsor Star*

GABLE, *The Globe and Mail*

— And don't forget your condoms!

CÔTÉ, *Le Soleil*, Quebec

CLEMENT, *The National Post*

DEWAR, *The Toronto Sun*

PETERSON, *The Vancouver Sun*

CORRIGAN, *The Toronto Star*

SARS and mad cow, the Canadian nightmare!

CÔTÉ, *Le Soleil*, Quebec

AISLIN, *The Gazette*, Montreal

CUMMINGS, *The Winnipeg Free Press*

DEA, *La Presse*, Montreal

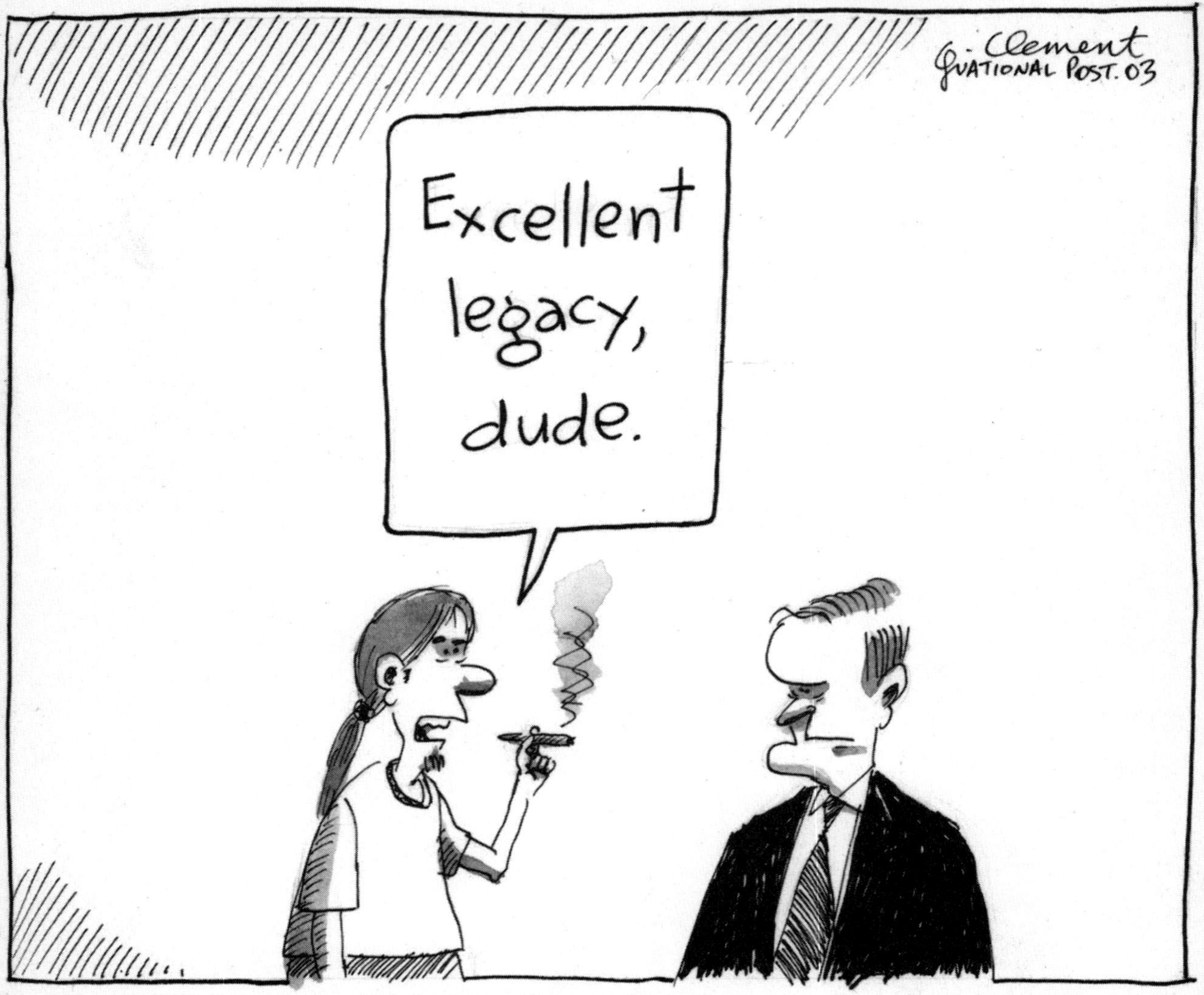
G. Clement
NATIONAL POST. 03
Excellent legacy, dude.

I pronounce your weed legal!

Chrétien tries to clear the air while the courts allow Canadians to light up.

This was definitely not Ralph Klein's year. Not only did the federal government sign the Kyoto Accord on climate change and promise to relax the law on marijuana consumption, but courts in Ontario and British Columbia also allowed homosexual couples to wed, prompting Klein to threaten to invoke the notwithstanding clause if all this became legal in Canada. Bishop Fred Henry of Calgary even condemned Jean Chrétien to eternal damnation if his government put same-sex marriage to a free vote in Parliament.

CORRIGAN, *The Toronto Star*

PASCAL, *The Gazette*, Montreal

CLEMENT, *The National Post*

PETERSON, *The Vancouver Sun*

MURPHY, *The Province*, Vancouver

AISLIN, *The Gazette*, Montreal

CORRIGAN, *The Toronto Star*

DE ADDER, *Halifax Daily News*

MAYES, *The Edmonton Journal*

CUMMINGS, *The Winnipeg Free Press*

What the legalization of same-sex marriage means

It means the end of everything that is normal and natural and regular and normal! (yikes)

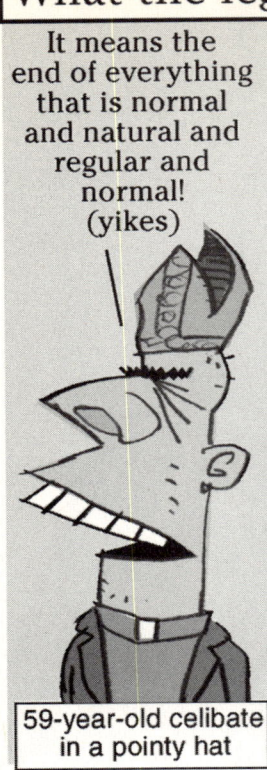

59-year-old celibate in a pointy hat

It means we are now pencilling Canada in between North Korea and Iran for a pre-emptive strike.

U.S. Secretary of Pre-Emptive Striking Donald Rumsfeld

It means Parliament is *finally* catching up with the courts.

It means when I have my mid-life crisis and ditch Gigi here for a twenty-something Gap salesgirl, I'm going to be paying alimony. (yikes)

murphy*the province

MURPHY, *The Province*, Vancouver

NOW THAT WE'RE LEGALLY MARRIED... I WANT A DIVORCE!

DEWAR, *Ottawa Sun*

GABLE, *The Globe and Mail*

ANDY, *The Globe and Mail*

GARNOTTE, *Le Devoir*, Montreal

ANDY, *The Globe and Mail*

.129

AISLIN '02
MONTREAL
THE GAZETTE
www.aislin.com

The long goodbye

The little guy from Shawinigan finally becomes the longest serving Liberal prime minister since Mackenzie King. Or is it Laurier? Anyway, it's definitely one of the two.

Jean Chrétien announced in the summer of 2002 that he would be leaving 18 months later. Seems there was always a reason to stick around. If not for the 40th anniversary of his first election, it was his last Commonwealth meeting, his 70th birthday or the 20th anniversary of Trudeau's retirement. By quitting on the last day of February of a leap year, he would ensure that his enemies could only celebrate his retirement every four years. Paul Martin, on the other hand, would be celebrating more often.

LEFCOURT

MOU, *The Toronto Star*

PETERSON, *The Vancouver Sun*

ANDY, *The Globe and Mail*

Chretien will leave in February 2004…
– I'm just killing time!

GARNOTTE, *Le Devoir*, Montreal

TAB, *The Calgary Sun*

DEA, *La Presse*, Montreal

GABLE, *The Globe and Mail*

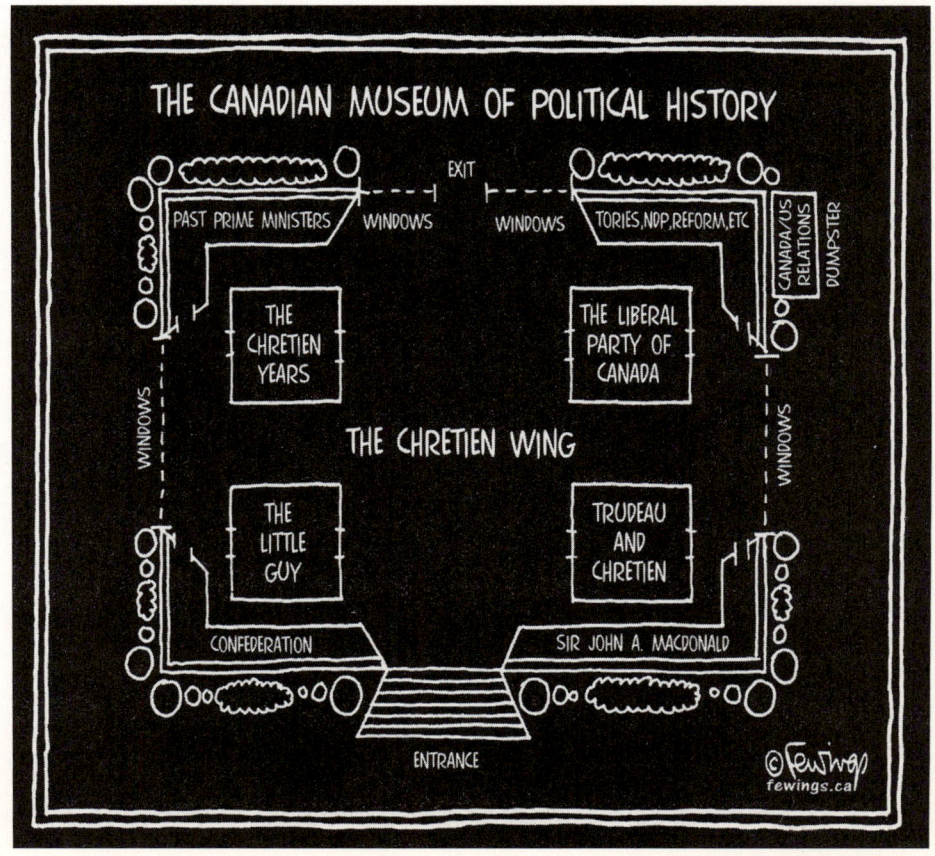

FEWINGS, *The Peterborough Examiner*

ANDY, *The Globe and Mail*

DE ADDER, *Halifax Daily News*

DOLIGHAN

John Manley speaks against royalty in Canada…
– Sorry, your Highness, I wasn't talking about you!

GARNOTTE, *Le Devoir*, Montreal

PETERSON, *The Vancouver Sun*

GRASTON, *The Windsor Star*

.141

GABLE, *The Globe and Mail*

MURPHY, *The Province*, Vancouver

TAB, *The Calgary Sun*

HARROP, *Back Bench*

KRIEGER, *The Province*, Vancouver

AISLIN is the name of TERRY MOSHER's eldest daughter and the *nom de plume* that he has used as the editorial page cartoonist for *The Gazette* in Montreal where he has worked since 1972. Mosher is also cartoon editor of *Maclean's*, Canada's national magazine. Part of his mandate includes increasing the national profile of young, aspiring Canadian cartoonists. He has produced thirty-five books, either collections of his own works or books that he has illustrated. Mosher also wrote a book with journalist Peter Desbarats entitled THE HECKLERS, a history of political cartooning in Canada that was published in 1980. The recipient of many awards, in May of 2003, Terry Mosher was appointed as an Officer of the Order of Canada. He is a member of the board of directors for The Old Brewery Mission, Montreal's largest homeless shelter.

aislin@thegazette.canwest.com

www.aislin.com
www.cagle.com

Born in 1952 in South Africa, DAVID ANDERSON (**ANDY**) was cartoonist for several newspapers in that country including *The Rand Daily Mail* until its closure in 1985 and then for *The Johannesburg Star*. He moved to Toronto with his wife and three sons in 1990, from where he continued to send back two editorial cartoons a week to The Star for the next 12 years. He currently freelances and his work has appeared regularly in *The National Post* and *The Globe and Mail* among others.

david@d-andersonillustration.com

www.d-andersonillustration.com

GRAHAME ARNOULD was born in Manhattan in 1958 and some 19 years later studied economics at Queen's University in Kingston, Ontario. Upon graduation he decided to become a cartoonist. On the strength of this work, he entered the world of advertising where almost all his best work involved cartoons. His ad work won awards in Canada, the U.S., Austria and Germany. He currently lives in Vancouver where he contributes weekly editorial cartoons and illustrations to *The Georgia Straight*. His gag cartoons are also distributed through the Cartoonists and Writers Syndicate in the U.S.

BADO is GUY BADEAUX's last name pronounced phonetically. Born in Montreal in 1949, he worked there for 10 years before moving to Ottawa in 1981 to become the editorial page cartoonist for *Le Droit*. Author of seven collections of his own work and winner of the 1991 National Newspaper Award, he serves as treasurer of the Association of Canadian Editorial Cartoonists.

bado@ledroit.com

www.artizans.com
www.cagle.com
www.vianetinfo.com

PAUL BORDELEAU was born in 1967. He started out as an illustrator working for advertising agencies before having a shot at caricature; first in *VOIR-Québec* in 1992, and then also for *VOIR-Outaouais*.

paul@bordeleau.qc.ca

www.bordeleau.qc.ca

Born in Montreal in 1945 and having studied painting and graphic arts at l'École des Beaux-Arts, **SERGE CHAPLEAU** became an instant celebrity in Quebec in 1972 with a weekly full colour caricature for *Perspectives*. He joined *Montréal Matin* two years later, where he did editorial cartoons until the paper folded following a long strike. After resurfacing at the very sedate *Le Devoir* in the mid- eighties, he has been at *La Presse* since April 1996 and is a four-time winner of the National Newspaper Award for Editorial Cartooning.

serge.chapleau@lapresse.ca

GARY CLEMENT was born in Toronto in 1959. Over the past ten years his illustrations have appeared in *The New York Times, The Wall St. Journal, The Boston Globe, The Globe and Mail, The Financial Post, The Washington Post, The Medical Post* and several other Posts. He has also written and illustrated two children's books: *Just Stay Put* (fall 96) and *The Great Poochini* (fall 99), which won the Governor General's Award for Illustration. Winner of four National Magazine Awards as well as awards from the Advertising & Design Club of Canada, *Applied Arts* magazine, American Illustration and The American Society of Newspaper Design. He lives in Toronto with his wife, two kids and various members of the animal kingdom.

gclement@nationalpost.com

www.nationalpost.com
www.cagle.com

Born in Toronto in 1951, **PATRICK CORRIGAN** studied fine arts at the Ontario College of Art, which led to a career of night-shift taxi driving. He forsook his extensive art training and freelanced for *The Financial Post, Maclean's* and *The Toronto Star.* He joined *The Star* in 1983 as a full-time illustrator, while filling in for Duncan Macpherson whenever possible. Twice nominated for a National Newspaper Award, he has won several awards in illustration and graphics (Society of Newspaper Design, New York Art Directors Club, Advertising Design Club of Canada, Toronto Art Directors Club). He was named the editorial page cartoonist in 1995 at *The Toronto Star* and can still quote you a return fare from the airport.

corrigan@thestar.ca

www.corrigan.ca
www.thestar.com
www.cagle.com

ANDRÉ-PHILIPPE COTÉ, born in 1955, has been the editorial cartoonist of *Le Soleil* since the summer of 1997. Author of the comic strip *Baptiste,* he has also worked for the humour magazine *Safarir* in the past decade. He has published seventeen books so far.

Born in 1948 in St. Thomas, Ontario, **DALE CUMMINGS** studied animation and illustration at Sheridan College in Oakville. During a brief stay in New York, he did some cartoons for *The New York Times.* He returned to Toronto in 1976, where he freelanced for *Last Post, Canadian Forum, Maclean's, The Toronto Star, Canadian Magazine* and *This Magazine.* Full-time editorial cartoonist with *The Winnipeg Free Press* since 1981, he won the National Newspaper Award in 1983.

www.artizans.com
www.cagle.com

PATRICK DEA was born in Montreal in 1965. Since 1984, his work has graced the pages of countless magazines and advertising. Formally caricaturist in the humour magazine *Safarir,* and more recently with *Kamikaz,* he now does two drawings a week for Montreal's daily *La Presse.* McDonald's, Coca-Cola and Loto-Québec are but a few in a long list of companies that have drawn on his talents. Musician in his spare time, he practises classical guitar.

patimage@ca.inter.net

www.portfolios.com/dea

Ils font un malheur...

... à Las Vegas   ... à Bagdad

MICHAEL DeADDER was born in Moncton, New Brunswick, in 1967. Full-time cartoonist at *The Halifax Daily News* since 2000, his work has appeared in various newspapers in Canada. After graduating from Mount Allison University in 1991, with a Bachelor of Arts degree in Fine Arts, he began working as an artist out of Halifax. Realizing that he needed food and shelter to survive, he sold editorial cartoons on the side. Eventually he began selling more editorial cartoons than paintings and a cartoonist was born. De Adder considers himself to be a failed painter rather than a successful cartoonist.

deadder@hfxnews.ca

www.hfxnews.ca
www.artizans.com
www.cagle.com

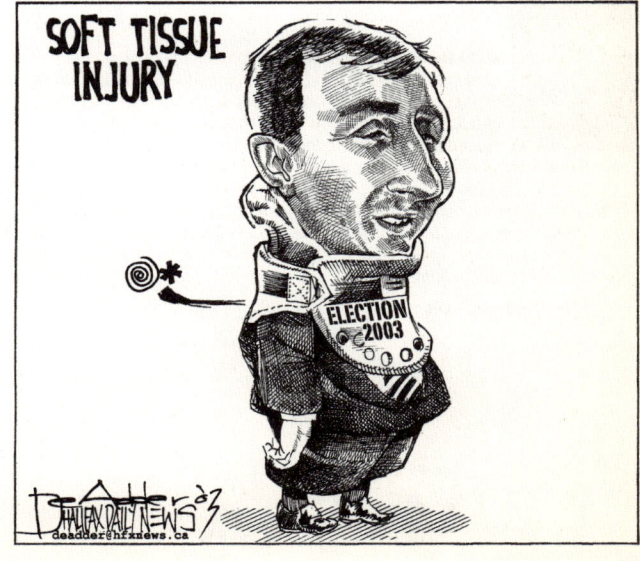

SOFT TISSUE INJURY

Born in Montreal in 1949, **SUSAN DEWAR** attended high school in Toronto, went to the University of Western Ontario in London, and graduated from Toronto Teachers' College. After working in commercial art in Toronto, she freelanced for *Canadian Forum, Teen Generation, Current* and *The Toronto Sun*. She joined The *Calgary Sun* as full-time editorial cartoonist in 1984 and won the 1987 National Business Writing Award for political cartooning. In October 1988 she became the editorial cartoonist of *The Ottawa Sun*. She is the mother of James Geoffrey.

sue.dewar@tor.sunpub.com

www.canoe.com/OttawaSun/dewar.html

DEWAR

TIM DOLIGHAN was born in 1966 and lives with his wife Mary and daughters Caili and Shanna and son, John, in Oshawa, Ontario. After receiving degrees from Laurier, York and Ottawa U (none of which had anything to do with art), he started freelancing and illustrating for community newspapers in 1992. Tim currently provides the daily editorial cartoon for Rogers hi-speed Internet. His work has received several national and Ontario community newspaper awards and is published across Canada in such publications as *The Toronto Sun*, *The Ottawa Citizen* and various Metroland papers.

tim@dolighan.com

www.cagle.com

: DOLIGHAN

JOHN FEWINGS was born in Simcoe, Ontario, in 1955. He began drawing caricatures of his high school teachers to piss them off and get laughs from his friends; it worked on both counts. His first editorial cartoons appeared in *The Port Dover Maple Leaf* and *The Simcoe Reformer*. He now resides in Peterborough with Gale, Josh and their Border collie, Buddy, working as a freelance graphic designer/cartoonist. His cartoons regularly appear in *The Peterborough Examiner*, *The Toronto Sun* and a number of other Canadian dailies.

john@fewings.ca

150.

THOMAS SZLUKOVENYI

Born in 1949 in Saskatoon, **BRIAN GABLE** studied fine arts at the University of Saskatche-wan. Graduating with a B.Ed. from the University of Toronto in 1971, he taught art in Brockville and began freelancing for the Brockville *Recorder and Times* in 1977. In 1980 he started full-time with the Regina *Leader-Post* and is presently the editorial cartoonist for *The Globe and Mail*. He has won National Newspaper Awards in 1986, 1995 and 2001.

bgable@globeandmail.ca

www.globeandmail.ca
www.cagle.com

FRANÇOIS DESAULNIERS

Born in Montreal in 1951, and after studies having nothing to do with drawing, MICHEL GARNEAU (**GARNOTTE**) has contributed to many newspapers and magazines in Montreal, including *CROC, TV Hebdo, Protégez-vous (Protect Yourself), Titanic* (of which he was editor-in-chief), *Les Expos, Je me petit-débrouille, La Terre de chez nous* and *Nouvelles CSN*. He became the editorial cartoonist for *Le Devoir* in April 1996.

garnotte@ledevoir.ca

www.ledevoir.com

MIKE GRASTON was born and raised in Montreal. He has been editorial cartoonist with the *Windsor Star* since 1980, after having spent time obtaining an honours degree in history from the University of Western Ontario and free-lancing for *The Ottawa Citizen*. His work has appeared in most Canadian newspapers as well as a number of American publications and has been featured on ABC's *Nightline*, CBC, CTV and *CBC Newsworld*. He has three daughters: Lisa, Carly and Raquel.

grastoon@cogeco.ca
mgraston@thestar.canwest.com

www.grastoon.com
www.cagle.com

Born in Liverpool, **GRAHAM HARROP** emigrated to Canada at the constant urging of friends, family and the British Government. He has worked in a mill, as a paint store clerk and once drove cab in a gorilla suit. He draws a comic strip for *The Globe and Mail* (*Back Bench*) editorial cartoons for *The Vancouver Sun* and, on Wednesdays, a fake moustache on his upper lip.

www.artizans.com
www.cagle.com

ANTHONY JENKINS was born in Toronto and spent his early career delivering *The Globe and Mail*. He joined the paper in 1974. In the 1980s he took three year long leaves of absence to travel in 74 countries. During the 1980s, he also began writing for the paper and continues today as a regular contributor. He draws caricatures at the *Globe* and still lives in Toronto with two daughters.

www.jenkinsdraws.com

BOB KRIEGER has actually managed to hold a job drawing editorial cartoons for *The Province* newspaper since 1981. Go figure. When he's not working, the Vancouver native likes to cook, eat, drink, play a little guitar and start rumours regarding the impending political comeback of Bill Vander Zalm... essentially anything to get out of doing yard work.

bkrieger@telus.net

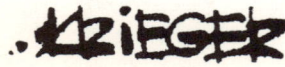

JACK LEFCOURT was born in 1964 in Kitchener, Ontario. He studied Fine Arts and History at the University of Waterloo where he also began his cartooning career, drawing campus-related panels for the student newspaper. His work has appeared in dailies, entertainment and community weeklies, and various magazines across Canada and elsewhere since he began drawing professionally in 1989. In the past three years, Lefcourt has developed an online web gallery of his work and has produced seven bound collections available through his site.

www.lefcourtland.com

Lefcourt

GARETH LIND, 39, has been cartooning for almost as long as he can remember. His satirical comic strip, *Weltschmerz*, has appeared in Toronto's *eye* weekly and other Ontario alternative papers since 1996. An additional political cartoon appears nationally in *This Magazine*. Lind is based in Guelph, Ontario, where he is a full-time, self-employed graphic designer. In between his drafting table and his computer, he catches a little life.

lind@lindtoons.com

www.weltschmerz.ca

LIND

CÉDRIC LOTH was born in Quebec in 1955. At eighteen years old, he worked as editorial cartoonist for *Le Devoir* in Montreal and *Le Soleil* in Quebec City before embarking on a career in France as a comic-strip artist for the famous magazine *Métal Hurlant* (*Heavy Metal*) in the early eighties. He would later work as copywriter and art director for major ad agencies in Quebec. In recent years Loth has returned to his first loves, comics and caricature. He directs animated series and is currently preparing an exhibition of his bronze sculptures.

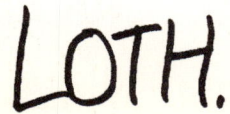

GRAEME MACKAY was born in Hamilton in 1968. After studying politics at the University of Ottawa, he flew off to England and sold bacon to famous people at a downtown London department store. When he nearly sliced his fingers off, he returned to Hamilton where he freelanced political caricatures. In 1997, he landed a job as editorial cartoonist for *The Hamilton Spectator*.

gmackay@hamiltonspectator.com

www.mackaycartoons.net
www.cagle.com

AGING SEA KING: PAST RETIREMENT

BRUCE MACKINNON grew up in Antigonish, Nova Scotia, studied fine arts at Mount Allison University, and was a member of the Graphic Design program at the Nova Scotia College of Art and Design. He started doing a weekly editorial cartoon with *The Halifax Herald* in 1985, working at home while raising his newborn daughter, Robyn. Through the miracle of day-care, he was able to join The *Herald* on a full-time basis in August of 1986. He has won several Atlantic Journalism Awards for editorial cartooning, was named "journalist of the year" in 1991, and was the National Newspaper Award winner for both 1992 and 1993.

bpmack@hfx.eastlink.ca

www.herald.ns.ca
www.artizans.com
www.cagle.com

GOOD TONY, GOOD. NOW GO MARK YOUR TERRITORY...

IRAQ

MALCOLM MAYES was born in Edmonton in 1962. Editorial cartoonist for *The Edmonton Journal* since June 1986, his work has appeared in most major Canadian newspapers and many major American newspapers, as well as numerous books and magazines including *Best Editorial Cartoons of the Year* (USA), *Reader's Digest*, and *The Great Big Book of Canadian Humour*. In addition, his cartoons have been featured on CBC, CNN, and at Montreal's International Museum of Humour.

mmayes@artizans.com

www.artizans.com
www.cagle.com

I'LL MISS DEBORAH GREY...

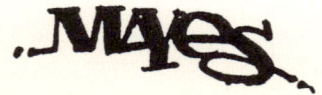

Toronto-born and old enough to know better, **CINDERS MCLEOD**'s achievements include degrees in art and television and filmmaking, a record on Billy Bragg's label, 10 years writing and cartooning for British newspapers, and a published book of her cartoon character, *Broomie Law* (Luath Press). She hasreturned to Canada after being adrift for 22 years (is that the year already?) along with Scottish newcomers Jules, Diarmid and Anya. Cinders currently works as an illustrator for *The Globe and Mail*. She is a political cartoonist because fighting injustice is the apple of her eye and newspaper ink is the rose of her nose.

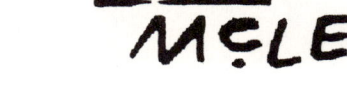

THEO MOUDAKIS (**MOU**) was born in Montreal in 1965 where he began freelancing for *The Gazette* in 1986. In 1991 he started full-time with *The Halifax Daily News* and in September 2000 became editorial cartoonist for *The Toronto Star*. His work has appeared in most Canadian dailies as well as *The New York Times*, *Time* and *Mad*, and has been three times short-listed for the National Newspaper Award.

mou@thestar.ca

www.thestar.com
www.artizans.com
www.cagle.com

DAN MURPHY was born in Missouri. He moved to Canada in the early seventies, drawing for various underground newspapers and aboveground magazines. He is a cartoonist and columnist for the Vancouver *Province*.

dmurphy@png.canwest.com

www.artizans.com

Born in 1955 in Woodbridge, Ontario, **STEVE NEASE** is art director of *The Oakville Beaver*, producing regular editorial cartoons and his family humour comic strip, *Pud*, which are both syndicated by Miller Features. Nease is a four-time recipient of the Canadian Community Newspapers Awards for cartooning. He and his wife Dian live in Oakville, and have four sons: Robert, Ben, Sam and Max.

snease@haltonsearch.com

PASCAL ÉLIE was born in Montreal in 1959. His cartoons are published twice a week (on Sundays and Mondays) in the Montreal *Gazette*. He's also the regular cartoonist for the business weekly *Les Affaires* and contributes to *Law Times* as well as for several other publications in Quebec and English Canada. He's been freelancing for a couple of decades, but left his day-job (as a legal editor) to become a full-time cartoonist in January 1998.

pascalelie@videotron.ca

GREG PERRY fell to earth in British Columbia during the '60s and learned to draw by studying prehistoric cave art. His history in newspaper is long and boring with many years spent at a variety of journals with no circulation. He was sued by the CEO of a public utility, made headlines for making Premier Bernard Lord cry and has been unanimously condemned by the New Brunswick legislature and various municipal councils. Now syndicated, Perry's cartoons appear daily across Canada.

perryink@rogers.com

DAVID NEEL

Winnipeg born, **ROY PETERSON** works for *The Vancouver Sun*. His work has appeared in all major Canadian and many American newspapers and magazines. He has produced many covers, illustrations and cartoons for *Maclean's*, including his 23-year association with Allan Fotheringham's Back Page column. His books include *The World According to Roy Peterson*, *Drawn & Quartered*, *The Canadian ABC Book* and the best-selling *Frog Fables and Beaver Tales* series with Stanley Burke. Recently widowed, Roy and Margaret raised five children. He has served as president of both the Canadian and American Associations of Editorial Cartoonists. Among his many citations he includes the Grand Prize at the Salon of Caricature in Montreal and seven National Newspaper Awards.

petersoninkinc@shaw.ca

www.artizans.com
www.cagle.com

JIM PHILLIPS was born in 1956, along with twin brother John, in Newmarket and raised in Jackson's Point, Ontario. Beginning his career in editorial cartooning at the age of 15 at *The Lake Simcoe Advocate*, he attended illustration and cartooning classes at Sheridan College and for a brief time studied at the Ontario College of Art. Winner of five Ontario and Canadian community newspaper awards for cartooning, he is the author of the daily cartoon (*SUNtoon*) published in *The Toronto Sun* since 1980 and syndicates his editorial cartoons through his website.

www.nationalheckle.com

INGRID RICE is a self-syndicated cartoonist published in over 50 markets across Canada and throughout British Columbia. Although she has not won any contests, she has appeared before the B.C. Press Council and been found to be reprehensible. Her free time is spent caring for assorted guinea pigs and a cat.

ouridea@home.com

DAVE ROSEN was born in Montreal in 1955 and started drawing for the alternative press at the age of 16. Over the years, he has contributed to *The Canadian Encyclopedia*, worked as a stand-up comic and been arrested for inciting a riot. He is currently a traffic reporter for CBC Radio and his cartoons appear in the *Montreal Mirror*. He has also published three books, none of which will be made into a movie.

toons@ca.inter.net

www.artizans.com
www.go.to/whathappened

R O S E N

FRED SEBASTIAN was born (in 1964) and bred in Ottawa. A graduate of Algonquin College's Commercial Art/Graphic Design program, his work appears in *Legion* and *The New York Times Book Review*. In 1994, he won a *Studio* magazine merit award for illustration and, in 2001, the National Press Club International Editorial Cartoon Competition On Press Freedom.

sebastian@magma.ca

www.artizans.com
www.reuben.org/sebastian

SHAHID MAHMOOD, born in 1971, grew up in Pakistan during General Zia's military rule. He started drawing for *The Star*, Karachi's evening newspaper at the age of 15. He went on to become the editorial cartoonist for both the national newspaper in Pakistan, *Dawn*, and newsmagazine, *Newsline*. A style described by editors as "irreverent and dark", his work has appeared in numerous Pakistani, North American and international publications and manages to continuously enrage Benazir Bhutto.

shahid@drawnconclusions.com

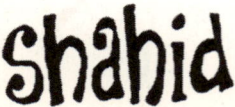

PHILIP STREET was born in Blyth, Ontario, in 1959. He studied English at the University of Toronto and, much later, animation at Sheridan College. His comic strip *Fisher* has appeared in The *Globe and Mail* since 1992. He lives in Toronto with his wife, Vanessa Grant.

pstreet@interlog.com

www.philipstreet.com

PHILIP STREET

TAB was born in Southern Prussia to a family of shepherds. Having survived the Industrial Revolution he came to Canada only to find the market for shepherds on the verge of collapse. Tab draws cartoons for *The Calgary Sun*.

www.canoe.com/CalgarySun/tab.html

MICHAEL ZAHARUK was born in Toronto in 1965. Graduating from the Ontario College of Art in 1991, he has been working as an illustrator and freelance editorial cartoonist ever since. His illustration work has been featured in *The Wall Street Journal*, *New York* magazine, *Saturday Night*, *The Globe and Mail* and *The Toronto Star*. In April 2003 he became the editorial cartoonist for *eye* weekly in Toronto.

zaharuk@sympatico.ca

www.artizans.com

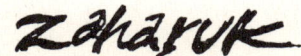

IN ADDITION TO PORTFOOLIO, HERE IS A LIST OF RECENT EDITORIAL CARTOON COLLECTIONS

BOWSER and BLUE, *The Canadian Illustrated Song Book*, illustrated by
    Aislin, with an introduction by Paul Martin, McArthur & Company.
CHAPLEAU, *L'année Chapleau 2003*, Boréal.
CÔTÉ, *De tous les Côté 2003*, Éditions Le Soleil.